PATRICK H. PERRINE

Unlocking Efficiency

*An Entrepreneur's Roadmap to Maximizing
Productivity and Personal Growth*

First edition

ISBN: 9798884749610

This book was professionally typeset on Reedsy.
Find out more at reedsy.com

DEDICATION

To the tireless trailblazers at the forefront of the entrepreneurial landscape—this book is dedicated to you. "Unlocking Efficiency" is a tribute to your unwavering commitment and relentless pursuit of excellence. May this guide serve as your compass and your companion as you navigate the exhilarating journey of entrepreneurship.

Warmly,
Patrick

"Success is not the key to happiness. Happiness is the key to success. If you love what you are doing, you will be successful."

— ALBERT SCHWEITZER

Contents

Preface

Welcome to 'Unlocking Efficiency: An Entrepreneur's Roadmap to Maximizing Productivity and Personal Growth,' the essential next step in the 'Be A Unicorn' series, designed to deepen the personal development and productivity strategies introduced in Step 7 of 'Unicorn Rising.' This volume is your comprehensive workbook, offering an interactive journey through the crucial aspects of personal growth and productivity that underpin entrepreneurial success.

In today's relentless entrepreneurial landscape, the intersection of personal growth with productivity is not just beneficial; it's essential. 'Unlocking Efficiency' is meticulously crafted to guide you through this intersection, providing the insights, strategies, and tools necessary for you to thrive amidst the challenges of entrepreneurship.

Drawing from two decades of entrepreneurial experience, this book delves into the heart of what it means to grow personally while enhancing your productivity. Each chapter is packed with actionable exercises, reflective questions, and real-world examples aimed at fostering a deeper understanding of yourself, optimizing your time management, and elevating your efficiency.

As part of the 'Be A Unicorn' series, 'Unlocking Efficiency' stands as a testament to the series' commitment to offering a holistic guide to entrepreneurial success. It builds on the foundation laid by previous volumes, ensuring a seamless continuation of your growth journey.

I invite you to dive into this book with a mindset ready for action and transformation. Engage with the exercises, apply the strategies to your entrepreneurial endeavors, and reflect on the insights to foster a personal and professional renaissance.

By the end of 'Unlocking Efficiency,' you will have crafted a personalized action plan that not only aligns with your entrepreneurial goals but also catalyzes your journey towards becoming a more productive, resilient, and self-aware entrepreneur.

Prepare to transform the insights gained from 'Unicorn Rising' into actionable strategies that will enhance your personal growth and skyrocket your productivity. Let's embark on this transformative journey together, unlocking the full potential of your entrepreneurial spirit through the power of personal development and efficiency.

Be A Unicorn: The New Entrepreneur's Ultimate Guide To Success

Dream It, Build It:
An Aspirational Odyssey Through
Entrepreneurship in Ten Inspiring Volumes.

Volume Seven

UNLOCKING EFFICIENCY
An Entrepreneur's Roadmap to Maximizing
Productivity and Personal Growth

1

Introduction to Personal Development

"The only true wisdom is in knowing you know nothing."
– Socrates

Personal development serves as the cornerstone for entrepreneurial excellence. In the world of entrepreneurship, where innovation meets execution, the journey toward success is both exhilarating and daunting. The path is strewn with challenges that test your limits, moments that demand your best, and opportunities that call for your unique contribution. Amidst this dynamic landscape, personal development emerges not just as a journey within but as a strategic component of entrepreneurial success. This chapter invites you on an exploration of the profound interconnection between personal growth and entrepreneurial achievement, providing insights into how cultivating your inner landscape can propel your business ventures to new heights.

The Essence of Entrepreneurship and Personal Development:

Entrepreneurship is often celebrated for its external accomplishments—innovations brought to market, businesses scaled, and industries transformed. Yet, at its core, entrepreneurship is deeply personal. It is a reflection of the individual's vision, resilience, and growth. Personal development, with its focus on enhancing one's skills, mindset, and overall well-being, is the silent engine driving this visionary force. It equips entrepreneurs with the tools to navigate uncertainty, lead with empathy, and create value that transcends the bottom line.

As we delve deeper into this exploration, we uncover the symbiotic relationship between personal development and entrepreneurial success. Like the two sides of a coin, they are distinct yet inseparable. Personal development fuels entrepreneurial endeavors with clarity, creativity, and resilience, while the entrepreneurial journey offers a unique platform for personal growth, pushing boundaries and revealing untapped potentials.

Opening Anecdote: Elon Musk: Visionary Ambition and the Quest for Knowledge

Consider Elon Musk, the trailblazer behind SpaceX and Tesla, whose relentless pursuit of personal development has not only expanded his knowledge across varied domains but also empowered him to confront ambitious challenges and secure monumental achievements.

Quick Thought:

Personal development is not just an optional accessory but the backbone of entrepreneurial success.

Entrepreneurship in Action: Key Ingredients

- **Commitment to Growth:** Embrace continuous learning as a lifelong journey, not a finite destination.
- **Self-Reflection:** Regularly assess your strengths and weaknesses to foster a deeper self-awareness.
- **Resilience:** Cultivate the tenacity to withstand setbacks and view challenges as opportunities for growth.

Case Study: Oprah Winfrey's Evolution into a Media Mogul

Background: Oprah Winfrey's journey from a humble beginning to becoming a global media leader showcases the transformative power of personal development. Facing adversity early in life, Oprah's relentless pursuit of growth, self-awareness, and resilience propelled her to the pinnacle of media and philanthropy.

Approach: Oprah's approach to personal development was multifaceted. She embraced continuous learning, seeking insights and knowledge not only in her professional field but also in personal wellness, spirituality, and leadership. By prioritizing self-reflection and emotional intelligence, Oprah cultivated a deep understanding of her audience, connecting with people on a profound level. Her commitment to authenticity and vulnerability became her strength, enabling her to build a media empire that resonates with millions globally.

Solution: Leveraging her insights into human emotions and stories, Oprah created a platform that went beyond traditional media. She introduced innovative formats in her show, focusing on storytelling, self-improvement, and empowerment. Her ability to discuss complex emotional and societal issues in an accessible manner transformed daytime television and contributed to the national conversation on critical topics.

Impact: Oprah's impact on the media industry and her audience is monumental. Through her work, she has inspired countless individuals to pursue personal growth and self-improvement. Her legacy includes not just her media achievements but also her contributions to education, philanthropy, and advocacy for women and children around the world.

Legacy and Insights: Oprah Winfrey's story exemplifies how personal development can lead to unparalleled success and influence. Her journey underscores the importance of self-awareness, resilience, and a commitment to growth. For entrepreneurs, Oprah's evolution offers valuable lessons in leveraging personal strengths and experiences to create a meaningful and impactful business.

Pro Tip: Cultivate a habit of daily reflection. Even a few minutes spent journaling or meditating on your experiences and lessons learned can dramatically enhance self-awareness and personal growth.

Exercise: Personal Growth Exploration

Self-Reflection for Deeper Self-Awareness:

1. **Journaling Exercise:** Dedicate 15 minutes each day to journal about your thoughts, feelings, and experiences. Focus on identifying patterns in your behavior and decision-making processes.
2. **Values Assessment:** List your top five values and reflect on how they align with your daily actions and decisions. Consider areas where you may need to realign your actions to better reflect your values.
3. **Feedback Solicitation:** Reach out to three individuals whose opinions you trust—be it mentors, peers, or family members. Ask for their honest feedback on your strengths and areas for improvement.

Goal Setting for Personal and Professional Growth:

1. **SMART Goals Identification:** Identify one personal and one professional goal using the SMART criteria. Write down the steps needed to achieve each goal.
2. **Vision Board Creation:** Build a vision board that represents your goals and aspirations. Use images, quotes, and symbols that resonate with your vision for the future.
3. **Accountability Partnership:** Partner with a friend or colleague to share your goals. Schedule regular check-ins to update each other on your progress and challenges.

Building Resilience and Embracing Growth:

1. **Resilience Reflection:** Reflect on a past challenge or failure. Write down what you learned from the experience and how it has contributed to your growth.
2. **Growth Mindset Affirmations:** Create a list of affirmations that promote a growth mindset. Repeat these affirmations daily to reinforce your commitment to personal development.
3. **New Skill Acquisition:** Choose a new skill to learn that aligns with your personal or professional growth goals. Dedicate a set amount of time each week to developing this skill.

Challenge For You: Over the next three months, focus on integrating these personal development exercises into your routine. Document your journey, noting the impact of these practices on your personal growth and entrepreneurial endeavors. Reflect on how the cultivation of self-awareness, goal setting, and resilience has influenced your approach to business and leadership.

Conclusion:

Personal development is the bedrock upon which entrepreneurial success is built. By dedicating ourselves to continuous growth, we not only enhance our capabilities and resilience but also set the stage for a thriving, innovative business. The journey towards self-awareness, self-reflection, and perpetual improvement is integral to unlocking our full potential as entrepreneurs.

Remember, the path of personal development is a marathon, not a sprint. Embrace this journey with open arms, and witness the transformative impact it will have on both your personal and professional life.

2

Self-Awareness and Self-Reflection

"Knowing yourself is the beginning of all wisdom."
— Aristotle

I n the entrepreneurial journey, self-awareness and self-reflection are not just tools but foundational pillars that support the entire edifice of personal and professional development. This chapter explores the profound importance of these elements in the context of entrepreneurship, presenting them as essential practices for anyone looking to navigate the complex waters of business with intention and insight. By cultivating a deep sense of self-awareness, entrepreneurs equip themselves to make decisions that are not only effective but deeply aligned with their personal values and long-term vision. It is this alignment that often spells the difference between mere success and fulfillment.

At the heart of entrepreneurship lies the challenge of continuous decision-making amidst uncertainty and constant change. It is here that self-awareness and self-reflection become invaluable. They enable entrepreneurs to understand their motivations, recognize their emotional responses, and assess their strengths and weaknesses with clarity. This level of introspection allows for a more nuanced approach to problem-solving and strategy development, ensuring that actions taken are not just reactive but rooted in a comprehensive understanding of both the self and the situation at hand.

Moreover, the practice of self-reflection fosters a culture of learning and adaptation, critical for any business's growth and sustainability. As entrepreneurs reflect on their experiences, successes, and failures, they uncover insights that drive innovation and improvement. This process of continual learning and self-discovery encourages a resilience that is indispensable in facing the inevitable challenges of entrepreneurship. It builds a framework within which entrepreneurs can grow not just as business leaders but as individuals, constantly evolving in response to their journey's demands.

This chapter aims to guide you through developing and nurturing your self-awareness and reflective practices. By doing so, you'll not only enhance your capacity to lead your venture more effectively but also embark on a path of personal growth that transcends the boundaries of your business. As we delve into the mechanisms through which self-awareness and self-reflection can be cultivated and applied, remember that the ultimate goal is to forge a path that is not only successful but meaningful and aligned with your deepest values and aspirations.

Opening Anecdote: Sara Blakely: Spanx's Journey from Idea to Empire

Sara Blakely, founder of Spanx, exemplifies the power of self-awareness in entrepreneurship. Starting with a simple idea and $5,000 in savings, Blakely's understanding of her own needs and gaps in the market led to the creation of a billion-dollar brand. Her journey underscores the value of knowing oneself and one's audience to innovate and thrive.

> **Quick Thought:**
> *Self-awareness illuminates the path to personal and professional growth, acting as a compass for entrepreneurial success.*

Entrepreneurship in Action: Key Ingredients

- **Introspection:** Regularly engage in self-reflection to understand your inner motivations and fears.
- **Feedback Integration:** Seek and thoughtfully consider feedback, viewing it as a tool for growth.
- **Continuous Learning:** Embrace a mindset of perpetual learning to adapt and evolve.

Case Study: Howard Schultz and Starbucks' Resurgence

Background: Howard Schultz's return to Starbucks as CEO in 2008 marked a pivotal moment for the company. Schultz's deep self-awareness and reflection on the company's core values and mission were instrumental in steering Starbucks back to its roots and reigniting its global success.

Approach: Schultz conducted open forums with employees, fostering a culture of transparency and mutual respect. This process not only demonstrated his self-awareness but also his commitment to embodying the values that made Starbucks a household name.

Solution: By realigning the company with its original ethos—focusing on customer experience and quality—Schultz revitalized the Starbucks brand. This strategic shift was a direct result of his self-reflection and understanding of the brand's strengths and weaknesses.

Impact: Starbucks saw a significant turnaround, with increased customer satisfaction and financial performance. Schultz's leadership and self-reflective approach paved the way for sustainable growth and innovation.

Legacy and Insights: Howard Schultz's story highlights the critical role of self-awareness and reflection in leadership. His ability to assess and realign the company's direction showcases the transformative power of these practices in achieving business success.

```
Pro Tip: Make self-reflection a routine practice.
Whether it's through meditation, journaling, or
strategic planning sessions, taking the time to
reflect on your actions and decisions is crucial for
growth.
```

Exercise: Navigating the Inner Landscape

Self-Reflection Journal:

1. **Daily Insights:** End each day by writing down three things you learned about yourself.
2. **Challenges and Solutions:** Note down challenges faced and how you addressed them, reflecting on what you might do differently in the future.
3. **Gratitude and Success:** Keep a record of what you are grateful for and your daily successes, no matter how small.

Feedback Loop Creation:

1. **Seek Constructive Feedback:** Regularly ask for feedback from peers, mentors, and team members.
2. **Reflect on Feedback:** Dedicate time to process the feedback received, identifying patterns and areas for improvement.
3. **Action Plan:** Develop an action plan based on feedback to enhance your strengths and work on weaknesses.

Mindfulness and Growth Mindset:

1. **Mindfulness Practice:** Incorporate mindfulness exercises into your daily routine to enhance self-awareness.
2. **Growth Challenges:** Set yourself small, achievable challenges to foster a growth mindset.
3. **Learning Reflections:** After completing a learning activity, reflect on what you learned and how it applies to your personal and professional life.

Challenge For You: Over the next month, focus on enhancing your self-awareness through these exercises. Document your journey, noting changes in your decision-making process, leadership style, and interpersonal relationships.

Conclusion:

Self-awareness and self-reflection are not just buzzwords; they are essential practices for any entrepreneur seeking to navigate the complex journey of business leadership. By understanding oneself deeply, entrepreneurs can lead with authenticity, make aligned decisions, and foster a culture of growth and innovation. As you continue to explore and reflect on your personal and professional identity, remember that this journey is one of continuous discovery and adaptation.

In the upcoming chapter, we'll dive into the art and science of goal setting and management, a critical component of translating self-awareness into actionable strategies for success.

3

Goal Setting and Goal Management

"A goal properly set is halfway reached."
— Zig Ziglar

In the realm of entrepreneurship, the ability to set clear and impactful goals is akin to charting a course in uncharted waters. This chapter explores the nuanced art of goal setting and the strategic discipline of goal management, key practices that transform the ethereal into the concrete. For the entrepreneur, goals do more than outline a desired future; they act as milestones on the path to success, imbuing daily tasks with purpose and direction. It is through the meticulous setting and managing of goals that entrepreneurs can translate their vision into actionable steps, thereby navigating the complex journey from concept to reality.

Effective goal setting and management serve as a dual beacon: one that illuminates the entrepreneur's immediate next steps and another that casts light on the distant horizon of their ultimate aspirations. This process begins with the articulation of one's vision, breaking it down into measurable, attainable objectives that collectively bridge the gap between where one stands today and where one aims to be. Moreover, it involves a continuous cycle of evaluation and adaptation, ensuring that goals remain relevant and responsive to the evolving business landscape.

But setting goals is only the beginning. Managing these goals to fruition demands perseverance, flexibility, and a keen awareness of one's progress. It requires entrepreneurs to maintain focus amid the myriad distractions and challenges that accompany the entrepreneurial journey, adapting their strategies in response to feedback and changing circumstances. This dynamic interplay between setting and managing goals not only propels entrepreneurs towards their desired outcomes but also fosters a growth mindset, encouraging continuous learning and personal development.

Opening Anecdote: Reid Hoffman: LinkedIn and the Blueprint for Professional Connectivity

Reid Hoffman, LinkedIn's co-founder, demonstrated the monumental power of goal setting when he envisioned transforming the professional landscape through networking. Hoffman's strategic goals for LinkedIn focused on creating unprecedented value for professionals worldwide, ultimately revolutionizing how we connect, job-hunt, and enhance our career paths.

> **Quick Thought:**
> *The clarity of purpose and direction that comes from effective goal setting is indispensable for entrepreneurial momentum and achievement.*

Entrepreneurship in Action: Key Ingredients

- **Vision Clarity:** Set goals that align with your overarching vision for both life and business.
- **Actionable Steps:** Break down each goal into manageable tasks to avoid overwhelm and maintain focus.
- **Adaptability:** Be prepared to adjust your goals as you progress, incorporating new insights and learnings.

Case Study: Airbnb's Strategic Pivots and Goal Realignment

Background: In its early days, Airbnb faced numerous challenges, from legal hurdles to market skepticism. The founders, Brian Chesky, Joe Gebbia, and Nathan Blecharczyk, set precise, adaptable goals that not only navigated these challenges but also capitalized on unexpected opportunities.

Approach: Airbnb's strategy included setting clear, measurable goals around user growth, market expansion, and user experience enhancements. They embraced flexibility, allowing them to pivot their goals in response to user feedback, regulatory landscapes, and competitive pressures.

Solution: One notable strategic goal was to enhance trust among users, leading to the introduction of features like verified photos and user reviews. These goals, rooted in improving the customer experience, significantly propelled Airbnb's growth and market acceptance.

Impact: By setting flexible yet targeted goals, Airbnb transformed from a niche room-sharing service into a global travel and experiences platform. Their goal-oriented approach enabled them to overcome initial obstacles and scale to new heights, fundamentally changing the travel industry.

Legacy and Insights: The Airbnb story underscores the importance of setting dynamic goals that can evolve with your business. It exemplifies how targeted, adaptable goals drive innovation, user engagement, and market penetration.

> Pro Tip: Regularly revisit and refine your goals. This practice ensures your objectives remain aligned with your evolving business landscape and personal growth trajectory.

Exercise: Crafting and Managing Your Blueprint for Success

Vision Mapping:

1. **Define Your Ultimate Vision:** Write a detailed description of your long-term vision for your business and personal life.
2. **Backward Planning:** Identify the key milestones needed to achieve this vision, working backward from the endpoint to the present.

SMART Goal Formulation:

1. For each milestone, specify clear, concise goals that define success.
2. Develop criteria for tracking progress toward each goal, ensuring they are quantifiable.

Milestone Celebration:

1. how you will celebrate reaching each milestone, reinforcing the value of accomplishment.
2. achieving a milestone, reflect on the journey, lessons learned, and adjustments needed moving forward.

Challenge For You: Over the next quarter, focus on one major goal that will significantly impact your business. Break this goal down into monthly milestones, apply the SMART criteria, and track your progress meticulously. Reflect on and celebrate each milestone achievement, adjusting your strategies as necessary based on what you learn.

Conclusion:

Effective goal setting and management are not just about achieving success; they're about defining it on your terms. By setting meaningful goals and managing them with intention, you can steer your entrepreneurial journey towards fulfilling your vision and purpose. Embrace the process of setting, pursuing, and achieving goals as a dynamic and continuous cycle that propels you and your business forward.

Coming up, we delve into mastering focus and concentration, essential skills for navigating the distractions of the modern world and channeling your efforts towards achieving your newly set goals.

4

Time Management Techniques

"Time is what we want most, but what we use worst."
— William Penn

Time, in the entrepreneurial journey, is a paradoxical commodity—abundantly available yet perpetually scarce. Effective time management transcends the conventional wisdom of productivity hacks; it is an essential discipline that enables entrepreneurs to align their daily actions with their highest priorities, ensuring that every moment is invested rather than merely spent. This chapter seeks to unravel the complexities of time management, offering entrepreneurs a toolkit for optimizing their most precious resource. It's about creating a life that balances the relentless demands of entrepreneurship with the personal pursuit of well-being and fulfillment.

For entrepreneurs, mastering time management is akin to mastering the art of navigation in the turbulent seas of business. It involves making strategic choices about where to focus energy and resources, determining what activities will propel the venture forward, and what tasks can be set aside or delegated. The essence of effective time management lies in the recognition that time, once passed, is irretrievable. This realization fosters a sense of urgency and intentionality, driving entrepreneurs to make conscious decisions about how to allocate their time to serve both their business and their personal life.

Moreover, time management is not solely about efficiency; it's equally about efficacy. It's about distinguishing the urgent from the important, focusing on actions that yield the highest value, and carving out space for innovation, creativity, and strategic thinking. This chapter will guide you through developing a time management system tailored to your unique entrepreneurial context, one that supports your goals, respects your personal commitments, and enhances your overall quality of life.

Opening Anecdote: Indra Nooyi: Mastering the Balance - Leading PepsiCo with Precision

Indra Nooyi, former CEO of PepsiCo, is renowned for her exceptional time management skills. Leading one of the world's largest companies, Nooyi balanced her professional responsibilities with personal commitments through meticulous planning and prioritization, demonstrating that effective time management is key to performing at an elite level in both personal and professional spheres.

> **Quick Thought:**
> *Mastery of time management enables entrepreneurs to navigate the demands of their bustling lives with grace and*

efficiency.

Entrepreneurship in Action: Key Ingredients

- **Strategic Prioritization:** Focus on what matters most to drive your vision forward.
- **Structured Planning:** Allocate your time with intention, ensuring that each action aligns with your broader objectives.
- **Flexibility:** Remain adaptable, ready to recalibrate your schedule as new priorities emerge.

Case Study: Buffer's Transparent Approach to Time Management

Background: Buffer, a social media management platform, has cultivated a culture where effective time management and work-life balance are paramount. Their open approach to remote work and flexible schedules has set a precedent in the tech industry for how time management can enhance productivity and employee satisfaction.

Approach: Buffer employs techniques like asynchronous communication and flexible work hours, allowing team members to manage their time according to personal productivity peaks and life commitments. This autonomy empowers individuals to schedule work when they feel most productive, rather than adhering to a strict 9-to-5 schedule.

Solution: By leveraging digital tools for project management and communication, Buffer ensures that all team members are aligned on tasks and deadlines, regardless of their physical location or time zone. This digital infrastructure supports their time management strategy, facilitating a seamless flow of information and collaboration.

Impact: Buffer's innovative time management approach has led to higher productivity levels, greater employee satisfaction, and the ability to attract top talent from around the globe. Their success demonstrates how flexible time management strategies can lead to substantial benefits for both employees and the organization.

Legacy and Insights: Buffer's story illustrates the transformative power of adopting flexible, employee-centric time management practices. It challenges traditional work models and offers valuable insights into how modern companies can navigate the complexities of time management in a digital age.

```
Pro Tip: Embrace digital tools to enhance your time
management strategies. The right technology can
simplify scheduling, automate tasks, and facilitate
better communication, freeing up valuable time to
focus on strategic priorities.
```

Exercise: Mastering Your Time

The Eisenhower Matrix, also known as the Urgent-Important Matrix, is a simple yet powerful tool for prioritizing tasks based on their urgency and importance. It helps individuals and teams focus on what truly matters by categorizing tasks into four quadrants:

1. **Urgent and Important (Quadrant I):** These are tasks that require immediate attention and are critical for your goals or deadlines. They're often associated with managing crises, meeting deadlines, and addressing pressing problems.

2. **Important but Not Urgent (Quadrant II):** Tasks in this quadrant are essential for long-term success and effectiveness but do not require immediate action. They include planning, relationship building, and personal growth activities. Focusing on these can reduce the number of tasks that become urgent and important.

3. **Urgent but Not Important (Quadrant III):** These are tasks that demand immediate attention but are not necessarily important for your long-term goals. They often involve dealing with other people's priorities, some emails, and some meetings.

4. **Neither Urgent Nor Important (Quadrant IV):** Tasks that fall into this category are typically distractions or time-wasters. They have little to no value and should be minimized or eliminated. These could include excessive social media use, irrelevant emails, or unnecessary meetings.

Using the Eisenhower Matrix helps individuals make strategic decisions about where to focus their time and energy, leading to improved productivity and a better balance between urgent tasks and important but not urgent tasks.

1. **Prioritization Matrix Creation:**

- Draft an Eisenhower Matrix to sort your tasks into four

categories: Urgent and Important, Important but Not Urgent, Urgent but Not Important, and Neither Urgent nor Important. Use this to guide your daily task prioritization.

- At the end of each day, reflect on the tasks you placed in each quadrant. Adjust your priorities for the next day based on what was or wasn't accomplished.

- Challenge yourself to delegate or eliminate at least one task from the Urgent but Not Important or Neither Urgent nor Important quadrants each day to focus more on what truly matters.

2. **Implementing Time Blocking:**

- Design a weekly schedule by assigning specific blocks of time for work tasks, personal activities, and rest. Ensure there's a balance that supports your overall well-being.

- Within your work blocks, dedicate specific times to deep-focus tasks and lighter, administrative tasks. Evaluate the effectiveness of these blocks at the end of the week.

- Introduce a flexible time block for unexpected tasks or overflow work. This helps manage unforeseen tasks without disrupting your planned schedule.

3. **Pomodoro Practice:**

- For one week, use the Pomodoro Technique by working for 25 minutes, then taking a 5-minute break. Keep track of how many "Pomodoros" it takes to complete various tasks.

- Experiment with extending the focus time to 50 minutes with a 10-minute break if the standard Pomodoro interval feels too short for deep work sessions.

- At the end of the week, assess the impact on your productivity and stress levels. Consider integrating or modifying the Pomodoro Technique based on your experience for ongoing time management improvement.

Challenge For You: Over the next month, commit to using the time blocking method to structure your days. Reflect weekly on the effectiveness of this approach and tweak your blocks as needed to maximize productivity and satisfaction.

Conclusion:

Effective time management is the linchpin of entrepreneurial efficiency and success. By adopting and adapting the strategies discussed, such as prioritization, time blocking, and the use of digital tools, you can significantly enhance your ability to manage time wisely. Overcoming common pitfalls like procrastination further unlocks your potential, enabling a more productive and balanced entrepreneurial journey.

As we move forward, the next chapter will introduce techniques to boost your focus and concentration, essential allies in the quest to make the most of your time.

5

Mindset and Resilience

"It's not that I'm so smart, it's just that I stay with problems longer."
— Albert Einstein

Navigating the entrepreneurial landscape requires more than just a brilliant idea or a groundbreaking product; it demands a mindset equipped to handle the inevitable hurdles and a resilience that fuels persistence in the face of adversity. This chapter explores the profound importance of cultivating a resilient mindset, which can often be the deciding factor between faltering at the first hurdle and persevering towards success. It's not merely about enduring challenges but embracing them as opportunities for growth and learning. For entrepreneurs, developing this resilience and a growth mindset is akin to arming themselves with an invisible shield, one that not only protects but empowers them to advance with confidence and determination.

The journey of entrepreneurship is marked by its highs and lows, successes and setbacks. Each entrepreneur's path is unique, yet all share the common challenge of navigating uncertainty. The cultivation of a resilient mindset and the practice of resilience are not just beneficial but essential in this high-stakes environment. They allow entrepreneurs to view setbacks not as insurmountable barriers but as integral stepping stones on the path to success. This perspective shift is crucial, transforming the way challenges are perceived and approached. It encourages a proactive stance towards problem-solving and innovation, rather than a reactive or defensive one.

Furthermore, the development of resilience and a growth mindset fosters an entrepreneurial spirit that is adaptable, flexible, and open to continuous learning. It underpins the ability to pivot strategies, explore new opportunities, and make calculated risks—all while maintaining a positive outlook and a steadfast commitment to one's vision. This chapter aims to guide you through the principles and practices that can help nurture these indispensable qualities. By embedding resilience and a growth-oriented approach into the fabric of your entrepreneurial endeavors, you equip yourself to tackle challenges head-on and emerge stronger, wiser, and more capable.

Opening Anecdote: J.K. Rowling: The Magic of Persistence in the World of Publishing

J.K. Rowling's journey to publishing the Harry Potter series is a testament to resilience and the power of a growth mindset. Facing rejection after rejection, Rowling persisted, fueled by belief in her story and her ability to improve as a writer. Her perseverance paid off, resulting in a world-renowned series and a legacy of imagination.

> **Quick Thought:**
> *A growth mindset and resilience transform obstacles into stepping stones toward success.*

Entrepreneurship in Action: Key Ingredients for Cultivating a Growth Mindset and Building Resilience

- **Persistence in the Face of Failure:** View each failure as a stepping stone towards your goals. Persistence isn't about ignoring the odds; it's about believing in your capacity to overcome them.
- **Adaptability to Change:** Embrace change as an inherent part of the entrepreneurial journey. Adaptability means pivoting with purpose, learning from new situations, and applying insights to future challenges.
- **Continuous Learning and Curiosity:** Foster an insatiable curiosity and a commitment to learning. Every interaction and experience is an opportunity to grow and expand your understanding and skills.

Case Study: Dyson's Persistence through Failure

Background: James Dyson's journey to creating the Dyson vacuum cleaner exemplifies resilience and a growth mindset. Dyson encountered 5,126 failures over 15 years as he worked to revolutionize vacuum technology with his cyclone design. Each failure was a lesson that brought him closer to success.

Approach: Embracing each setback as an opportunity to learn, Dyson meticulously analyzed each failure to improve his design. His commitment to innovation and refusal to give up, despite numerous challenges, underscored his growth mindset.

Solution: Dyson's persistence paid off with the creation of the first bagless vacuum cleaner that changed the industry. His ability to persist through thousands of failures and maintain belief in his vision was instrumental in his success.

Impact: Today, Dyson Ltd is a global technology company with a wide range of innovative products. Dyson's story demonstrates how resilience, paired with a growth mindset, can lead to groundbreaking achievements.

Legacy and Insights: Dyson's journey teaches us that behind most innovations are countless unseen failures. It's the entrepreneur's mindset and resilience in the face of these failures that can turn a simple idea into a revolutionary product.

```
Pro Tip: Regularly reflect on challenges you've
overcome in the past. This reflection strengthens
your resilience muscle and prepares you for future
obstacles.
```

Exercise: Cultivating Growth and Resilience

Embracing Challenges:

1. Write down a current challenge you are facing in your entrepreneurial journey.
2. Outline steps to tackle this challenge, viewing it as an opportunity for growth.
3. After implementing your plan, reflect on the experience.

What did you learn? How can you apply this learning in the future?

Learning from Setbacks:

1. Choose a recent setback and document what happened. Be as detailed as possible.
2. What can you learn from this setback? Identify at least three key insights.
3. How will you apply these lessons to future challenges? Outline actionable steps.

Building a Supportive Network:

1. Make a list of individuals who inspire you or from whom you can learn. Aim for a mix of peers and more experienced mentors.
2. Contact at least one person from your list this month for advice or feedback on a specific issue you're facing.
3. Consider how you can offer value back to your network. This could be through sharing your own experiences, offering support, or connecting individuals with mutual interests.

Challenge For You: For the next 90 days, focus on one area of growth mindset or resilience you wish to develop. Apply the exercises above, tracking your progress weekly. Document not just your actions, but also your mental and emotional responses to these exercises. At the end of the period, evaluate how these practices have impacted your approach to entrepreneurship and personal growth.

Conclusion:

The entrepreneurial path is inherently fraught with challenges. However, it's the mindset and resilience we cultivate that dictate our journey's trajectory. By embracing a growth mindset, viewing failures as lessons, and building our resilience, we prepare ourselves to navigate the entrepreneurial landscape with confidence and grace.

6

Stress Management and Work-Life Balance

"It's not the load that breaks you down, it's the way you carry it."
— Lena Horne

Navigating the entrepreneurial landscape requires more than just business acumen; it demands a delicate balance between professional drive and personal well-being. The journey of entrepreneurship is inherently filled with pressures, deadlines, and challenges that can easily lead to stress and burnout if not managed properly. Yet, amidst these demands, lies the crucial task of maintaining a healthy equilibrium between relentless professional pursuits and the inherent need for personal well-being. This chapter is dedicated to unraveling the complexities of stress management and the art of achieving work-life balance. It's designed to guide entrepreneurs through the process of transforming potential stressors into catalysts for growth and productivity, all while preserving the essence of personal happiness and fulfillment.

In the fast-paced world of business, where time is a currency and productivity a measure of success, it's easy to overlook the significance of balance and well-being. However, history and research consistently show that long-term success is built on a foundation of sustainable practices, including effective stress management and a commitment to work-life harmony. Entrepreneurs, therefore, must learn not just to survive but to thrive amid the pressures of their endeavors by adopting strategies that promote resilience, efficiency, and personal satisfaction.

This exploration into stress management and work-life balance is not just about avoiding burnout; it's about creating a lifestyle that enhances creativity, encourages strategic thinking, and fosters meaningful connections. It's about recognizing that the well-being of the entrepreneur is intrinsically linked to the health of the business. By prioritizing these aspects, entrepreneurs can unleash their full potential, not by doing more, but by being more strategic, mindful, and balanced in their approach to both life and work.

Opening Anecdote: Arianna Huffington: Redefining Success Beyond the Grind

Arianna Huffington, co-founder of The Huffington Post, experienced a wake-up call after collapsing from exhaustion, which led her to advocate for the importance of work-life balance and well-being in the corporate world. Her journey underscores that success doesn't have to come at the expense of health and happiness.

> ***Quick Thought:***
> *Effective stress management and achieving work-life balance are not perks but necessities for entrepreneurial success and longevity.*

Entrepreneurship in Action: Key Ingredients

- **Mindful Prioritization:** Recognize that being busy isn't the same as being productive. Focus on what truly moves the needle for your business and personal growth.
- **Strategic Delegation:** Understand that you can't—and shouldn't—do everything yourself. Delegating tasks effectively allows you to focus on your strengths and high-impact activities.
- **Intentional Recharging:** Regularly scheduled downtime is not a luxury; it's essential for creativity, problem-solving, and sustained energy levels.

Case Study: Google's Work-Life Balance Initiatives

Background: Google has long been celebrated for its commitment to employee well-being and work-life balance. The tech giant implements various programs and policies designed to reduce stress and promote a healthy work-life integration among its employees.

Approach: Google offers its workforce access to wellness programs, flexible work hours, and the freedom to pursue passion projects. These initiatives are rooted in the understanding that employee well-being directly impacts creativity, productivity, and job satisfaction.

Solution: By institutionalizing work-life balance practices, Google not only enhances employee well-being but also sets a benchmark in the tech industry for attracting and retaining top talent.

Impact: Google's focus on work-life balance has contributed to its reputation as one of the best places to work, highlighting how prioritizing employee well-being can lead to business success and innovation.

Legacy and Insights: Google's practices demonstrate that fostering an environment where work-life balance is achievable and encouraged can result in a more motivated, productive, and innovative workforce.

```
Pro Tip: Start small with work-life balance
initiatives in your own enterprise. Even simple
changes, like encouraging regular breaks or offering
flexible working hours, can have a significant impact
on team morale and productivity.
```

Exercise: Building Your Stress Management and Work-Life Harmony

Self-Care Strategies:

1. Incorporate at least 30 minutes of exercise into your daily routine to boost mood and reduce stress.
2. Dedicate 10 minutes each day to mindfulness or meditation to enhance focus and clarity.

3. Commit to a regular sleep schedule, aiming for 7-9 hours of quality sleep per night to rejuvenate your body and mind.

Time Management Mastery:

1. For one week, track how you spend your time. Identify activities that don't contribute to your goals and consider minimizing or eliminating them.
2. Practice saying no to requests or opportunities that don't align with your priorities or values.
3. Spend 10 minutes each morning planning your day, focusing on tasks that align with your key goals and personal well-being.

Stress Reduction Techniques:

1. Use deep breathing techniques to center yourself during stressful moments.
2. Each night, write down three things you're grateful for to shift focus away from stress and towards positivity.
3. Allocate specific times to disconnect from digital devices, reducing information overload and increasing mental space.

Challenge For You: Implement one new strategy from each of the above sections into your daily routine for the next month. Observe and journal the effects on your stress levels, productivity, and overall well-being.

Conclusion:

Stress management and work-life balance are not merely aspirational goals; they are essential practices for any entrepreneur aiming for both professional success and personal fulfillment. By embracing these strategies, entrepreneurs can build a foundation of resilience, well-being, and sustained performance, turning challenges into opportunities for growth. As we move forward, remember that the journey of entrepreneurship is a marathon, not a sprint, requiring careful attention to one's well-being and balance.

In the next chapter, we'll delve into productivity hacks and tools that can further enhance your efficiency and effectiveness, paving the way for even greater achievements in your entrepreneurial journey.

7

Productivity Hacks and Tools

"Do not squander time, for that's the stuff life is made of."
— Benjamin Franklin

Navigating the entrepreneurial landscape demands more than just hard work; it requires strategic efficiency and a mastery of productivity. In the entrepreneurial journey, the true measure of productivity lies not in the number of hours worked but in the quality and impact of those hours. This chapter aims to equip you with an arsenal of productivity hacks and tools designed to amplify your efficiency, streamline your operations, and elevate the effectiveness of your daily routines. As entrepreneurs, the quest for productivity is a continuous one, with the landscape ever-evolving. Adopting the right strategies and leveraging cutting-edge tools can dramatically transform your approach to work, enabling you to achieve more in less time and with less effort.

The pursuit of productivity is more than a quest for efficiency; it's about crafting a work-life synergy that balances ambition with well-being. It challenges the conventional wisdom that busier is better, advocating instead for a smarter, more intentional approach to business and personal tasks. In this digital age, where distractions are plentiful and demands on our time are incessant, mastering the art of productivity has become more crucial than ever. It's about making informed choices—deciding not just what to do but what not to do, and when and how to do it most effectively.

This exploration into productivity hacks and tools is grounded in the principle that optimizing your workflow doesn't just enhance your business outcomes; it enriches your life. By freeing up time and mental space, you open doors to creativity, innovation, and perhaps most importantly, moments of rest and rejuvenation. The strategies discussed in this chapter are not one-size-fits-all solutions but starting points for you to customize and integrate into your unique entrepreneurial blueprint. From harnessing technology to declutter your digital life to adopting mindfulness practices that sharpen your focus, each hack and tool is a step towards a more productive, balanced, and fulfilling entrepreneurial experience.

Opening Anecdote: Tim Ferriss: Rethinking Productivity with the 4-Hour Philosophy

Tim Ferriss, author of "The 4-Hour Workweek," transformed the concept of productivity by challenging the traditional 9-to-5 grind. His experimental approach to lifestyle design and productivity hacks, such as outsourcing and batching tasks, illustrates the potential to achieve more with less, emphasizing effectiveness over busyness.

> **Quick Thought:**
> *Productivity isn't merely about filling every moment with tasks; it's about selecting the right tasks and executing them with precision and purpose.*

Entrepreneurship in Action: Key Ingredients

- **Intentional Focus:** Zero in on tasks that align with your core mission and delegate or eliminate the rest.
- **Streamlined Processes:** Adopt systems and tools that automate or simplify repetitive tasks, freeing up mental space for creative thinking.
- **Continuous Optimization:** Regularly review and refine your productivity strategies to adapt to changing circumstances and capitalize on new efficiencies.

Case Study: The Zappos Approach to Enhancing Employee Productivity

Background: Zappos, the online shoe and clothing retailer known for its exceptional customer service, also excels in creating a productive and happy work environment. Their focus on company culture and employee satisfaction underscores their innovative approach to productivity.

Approach: Zappos encourages employees to take ownership of their time and tasks, fostering an environment where autonomy and accountability go hand in hand. They implement flexible scheduling and offer various personal development opportunities, believing that a fulfilled employee is a productive one.

Solution: By placing trust in their employees and providing them with the resources and flexibility to manage their work, Zappos has cultivated a highly engaged and efficient workforce. Their emphasis on culture and employee well-being has proven to be a powerful driver of productivity.

Impact: Zappos' productivity philosophy has not only contributed to its reputation for exceptional service but also to its significant business achievements. Their approach demonstrates how prioritizing employee satisfaction and empowerment can lead to increased productivity and business success.

```
Pro Tip: Embrace the philosophy that productivity
tools and hacks should serve you, not enslave you.
Regularly assess the effectiveness of your tools and
be willing to make changes to keep your workflow
optimized.
```

Exercise: Crafting Your Productivity Blueprint

Environment Optimization:

1. Tailor your workspace to inspire and enable focus. This might include ergonomic adjustments, motivational items, or noise-cancellation devices.
2. Dedicate time to declutter your digital workspace. Organize files, streamline your inbox, and tidy your desktop to minimize distractions.

3. Integrate plants or position your desk to maximize natural light, enhancing well-being and focus.

Prioritization Mastery:

1. Each morning, identify and write down the three most critical tasks that will drive the most value for your day.
2. At the week's end, review your accomplishments and identify areas for improvement. Adjust your priorities as needed.
3. Practice declining requests or opportunities that don't align with your highest priorities. Saying no frees up space for tasks that matter most.

Leveraging Automation:

1. Set up filters and rules in your email client to automatically sort, prioritize, or archive incoming emails.
2. Use scheduling tools like Calendly to automate meeting bookings, avoiding the back-and-forth of finding suitable times.
3. Group similar tasks together and schedule them in dedicated blocks to reduce context switching and enhance focus.

Challenge For You: Implement one new productivity strategy each week from the list above. Keep a journal of your experiences, noting which strategies enhance your productivity and which ones might need tweaking.

Conclusion:

Embracing productivity is about intelligently navigating the demands of entrepreneurship with grace and strategic acumen. By prioritizing effectively, embracing automation, and creating an environment conducive to focus, you can unlock a level of productivity that propels your entrepreneurial endeavors forward. Let the insights and strategies from this chapter serve as your compass in the relentless pursuit of efficiency and excellence.

8

Building Habits for Success

"The secret of your future is hidden in your daily routine."
— Mike Murdock

Success is not an overnight achievement—those small, repeated actions that, over time, shape our destiny. Habits are the invisible architecture of daily life, accounting for nearly half of our behaviors. In the world of entrepreneurship, where every decision and action can pivot the direction of one's journey, the role of habits becomes undeniably central. This chapter aims to illuminate the profound influence that well-crafted habits can exert on an entrepreneur's path to success. By delving into the science of habit formation and offering practical strategies for building effective habits, we seek to empower entrepreneurs with the tools to mold their futures through deliberate daily actions.

The cultivation of beneficial habits is akin to planting seeds of future triumphs. Just as a gardener tends to their garden, ensuring the right conditions for growth, entrepreneurs must nurture their habits with intention and care. The process of habit formation is both an art and a science, requiring an understanding of the psychological triggers that initiate behaviors, the routines themselves, and the rewards that sustain them. Through strategic habit formation, entrepreneurs can systematically enhance their productivity, creativity, and resilience, paving the way for sustained success and well-being.

Moreover, the journey of embedding new habits or re-shaping old ones is deeply personal and reflective, offering entrepreneurs a mirror to their motivations, challenges, and as-pirations. It is a journey that transcends mere business strategy, touching the core of personal growth and self-discovery. This chapter not only explores the mechanics of habit formation but also encourages a holistic approach to personal and professional development, highlighting the interconnectedness of individual habits with the larger tapestry of entrepreneurial success.

Opening Anecdote: Stephen King: The Discipline Behind a Literary Giant

Stephen King, one of the most prolific authors of our time, attributes his enormous output to a simple set of writing habits. Every day, King commits to writing 2,000 words, maintaining a routine that has resulted in over 60 novels. This discipline showcases the profound impact that consistent habits can have on productivity and success.

> **Quick Thought:**
> *The foundation of success is built not on sporadic acts of greatness but on the daily habits that accumulate over time.*

Entrepreneurship in Action: Key Ingredients

- **Consistent Application:** Success comes from the daily application of small, manageable tasks that align with your broader goals.
- **Goal Alignment:** Ensure that each habit you cultivate directly contributes to your entrepreneurial objectives, enhancing your focus and direction.
- **Adaptability:** Be willing to adjust your habits as your goals and circumstances evolve, maintaining flexibility in your approach to success.

Case Study: The Habit-Driven Success of Canva

Background: Melanie Perkins, CEO and co-founder of Canva, leveraged the power of habit to transform a simple idea into a graphic design powerhouse. The journey of Canva is a testament to how persistent habits and relentless focus can turn visions into reality.

Approach: From its inception, Canva's team cultivated habits of continuous learning, user-focused design iterations, and relentless pursuit of excellence. Perkins encouraged a culture where feedback loops and data-driven decisions became routine, enabling rapid growth and adaptation.

Solution: By embedding these habits into the company's DNA, Canva has continuously evolved, staying ahead of market trends and expanding its offerings to meet the growing needs of its users.

Impact: Today, Canva is a multi-billion dollar company, used by millions worldwide. Its success story underscores the cumulative power of daily habits in achieving entrepreneurial success.

> Pro Tip: Identify one keystone habit that can serve
> as a catalyst for change in your life and business.
> Focus on embedding this habit deeply into your
> routine, and watch as it begins to influence other
> areas of your life positively.

Exercise: Cultivating Success-Driven Habits

Habit Identification:

1. Identify habits that will most impact your entrepreneurial success.
2. For each habit, write down how it contributes to your goals.
3. Choose one habit to focus on based on its potential impact.

Implementation Strategy:

1. Divide your chosen habit into small, actionable steps.
2. Determine a specific time and cue for your habit. Integrate it into your existing routine.
3. Keep a habit tracker to monitor your consistency and progress.

Adjustment and Optimization:

1. At the end of each week, review your habit tracker and

identify any challenges.

2. Make necessary adjustments to your strategy to overcome identified obstacles.

3. Once your initial habit is firmly established, repeat the process with another prioritized habit.

Challenge For You: Commit to developing your chosen habit over the next 66 days—the average time it takes to form a new habit according to research. Document your journey, noting the challenges, successes, and insights gained.

Conclusion:

The alchemy of habit transformation lies in the consistent repetition of small actions aligned with your entrepreneurial aspirations. Like Stephen King's unwavering commitment to his craft, let your daily habits be the building blocks of your success. By understanding the habit loop, focusing on keystone habits, and applying strategic habit formation techniques, you can create a framework for lasting achievement and fulfillment.

9

Personal Growth and Continuous Learning

"Live as if you were to die tomorrow. Learn as if you were to live forever."
— *Mahatma Gandhi*

Entrepreneurship is not merely a business endeavor; it is a journey of relentless personal development and lifelong learning. This chapter is dedicated to unraveling the profound impact that continuous self-improvement and the acquisition of new knowledge have on an entrepreneur's ability to innovate, adapt, and lead. In an age where change is the only constant, the capacity to grow personally and intellectually becomes the cornerstone of sustainable success and leadership in any field.

At the heart of every successful entrepreneur lies an unwavering commitment to personal growth and an insatiable curiosity for learning. This dual pursuit not only enriches one's life but also amplifies their impact on their business and the broader community. By embedding personal growth and continuous learning into the DNA of their entrepreneurial ventures, leaders can navigate the complexities of the modern business world with confidence and foresight. It is through this lens of ongoing development that entrepreneurs can transform challenges into opportunities, fostering innovation and driving forward with a vision that transcends the present.

Understanding oneself, embracing change, and persistently seeking knowledge are practices that fuel the entrepreneurial spirit and catalyze profound transformations. Whether it's enhancing leadership skills, mastering new technologies, or deepening market insights, the journey of personal growth and continuous learning is endless. This chapter aims to inspire and equip entrepreneurs with the mindset and tools necessary to embark on this journey, highlighting the indelible link between individual development and entrepreneurial excellence.

Opening Anecdote: Oprah Winfrey: From Talk Show to Thought Leader

Oprah Winfrey's journey from a humble beginning to becoming a global media mogul and philanthropist exemplifies the essence of personal growth and continuous learning. Her insatiable appetite for knowledge, reflected in her well-known book club and leadership seminars, highlights how lifelong learning is integral to personal and professional success.

> **Quick Thought:**
> *The journey of personal growth and continuous learning is not a luxury but a necessity for the modern entrepreneur.*

Entrepreneurship in Action: Key Ingredients

- **Curiosity:** Foster an unyielding curiosity about your industry, emerging technologies, and the world around you.
- **Resilience:** Use setbacks as a springboard for growth, approaching each challenge as a learning opportunity.
- **Reflection:** Regularly reflect on your experiences, distilling actionable insights to guide future decisions.

Case Study: Satya Nadella's Transformation of Microsoft

Background: Satya Nadella took the helm at Microsoft during a period of stagnation. His leadership, characterized by an emphasis on growth mindset, reinvigorated the company's culture and business strategy.

Approach: Nadella encouraged employees to shift from a know-it-all to a learn-it-all mentality. This cultural transformation empowered teams to experiment, embrace failure as a learning opportunity, and innovate more freely.

Solution: By fostering an environment where learning from mistakes was not only accepted but encouraged, Microsoft saw a resurgence in creativity, collaboration, and technological advancement.

Impact: Microsoft's renewed focus on cloud computing and AI, driven by this cultural shift, has reestablished its position as a tech powerhouse. Nadella's leadership underscores the transformative power of personal growth and continuous learning in revitalizing a global corporation.

Pro Tip: Make learning a daily habit. Whether it's reading an article, listening to a podcast, or taking an online course, dedicate a portion of your day to acquiring new knowledge.

Exercise: Fostering Your Growth

Learning Plan:

1. Identify key areas where enhancing your skills could significantly impact your business.
2. Compile a list of books, courses, and other resources relevant to your goals.
3. Block out a daily time slot dedicated to learning.

Networking for Growth:

1. Commit to attending or participating in at least one industry event each quarter.
2. Seek out a mentor or advisor who can provide guidance and insight.
3. Join or form a mastermind group with fellow entrepreneurs.

Reflective Practice:

1. Maintain a daily or weekly journal to reflect on your learning and experiences.

2. Regularly solicit feedback from peers, mentors, and customers.
3. Use insights from reflection and feedback to refine your approach and strategies.

Challenge For You: Over the next 90 days, implement your learning plan. Track your progress and note any shifts in your mindset, capabilities, or business outcomes as a result of your dedicated learning and reflection.

Conclusion:

Embarking on a path of personal growth and continuous learning equips entrepreneurs with the agility, knowledge, and insight needed to excel. As demonstrated by leaders like Satya Nadella, cultivating a culture of learning can transform organizations and lead to unprecedented success. Embrace this journey with an open heart and mind, and let the endless pursuit of knowledge illuminate your path to achievement.

10

Building a Supportive Environment

"My mission in life is not merely to survive, but to thrive; and to do so with some passion, some compassion, some humor, and some style."
— Maya Angelou

Embarking on the entrepreneurial journey can often feel like navigating a ship through the vast and sometimes stormy seas of the business world. The quality of the wind that propels this ship forward—be it a gentle breeze or a guiding gale—is largely derived from the environment we cultivate around us. Such an environment, rich in support, inspiration, and resources, acts as a beacon of light, guiding entrepreneurs through uncharted territories towards the shores of success. This chapter seeks to illuminate the fundamental aspects of creating a nurturing ecosystem that not only sustains entrepreneurs through their ventures but also amplifies their capacity to achieve and exceed their goals.

At the core of every thriving entrepreneur lies a carefully woven network—a tapestry of mentors, collaborators, supporters, and even adversaries, each contributing to the richness of the entrepreneurial experience. It's in the diversity of these relationships and the quality of interactions that entrepreneurs find the resilience to persevere, the courage to innovate, and the wisdom to navigate the complexities of their industries. By delving into strategies for nurturing such relationships and creating environments conducive to growth, this chapter provides a blueprint for entrepreneurs to construct their unique supportive ecosystems, laying a solid foundation for their endeavors.

A supportive environment transcends the physical workspace, encompassing the emotional, intellectual, and social realms that influence an entrepreneur's journey. It's about creating spaces—both literal and metaphorical—that foster creativity, encourage risk-taking, and celebrate successes while providing a safety net for inevitable failures. This holistic approach to building a supportive environment is instrumental in shaping not just successful businesses but fulfilled entrepreneurs who can enjoy the journey as much as the destination.

Opening Anecdote: Richard Branson: Building Success Through Community

Richard Branson, the visionary behind the Virgin Group, attributes much of his success to the vibrant, supportive community he's built around him. From mentors to peers, and even competitors, Branson's network is a testament to the power of cultivating relationships that challenge, inspire, and elevate.

> **Quick Thought:**
>
> *A supportive environment isn't a luxury; it's a cornerstone of entrepreneurial resilience and success.*

Entrepreneurship in Action: Key Ingredients

- **Empathy and Understanding:** Foster relationships rooted in empathy, ensuring mutual support and understanding amidst the entrepreneurial rollercoaster.
- **Diversity of Thought:** Encircle yourself with individuals from varied backgrounds and expertise, enriching your perspective and driving innovation.
- **Shared Growth:** Commit to the collective growth of your network, believing in the principle that a rising tide lifts all boats.

Case Study: The Pixar Braintrust

Background: Pixar Animation Studios, renowned for its string of blockbuster films, credits a significant part of its success to the 'Braintrust'—a group of creatives who provide candid, constructive feedback on each other's work without any authority over it.

Approach: This unique assembly thrives on transparency, mutual respect, and a shared commitment to excellence. It embodies a supportive environment where creative ideas are nurtured, and constructive criticism is welcomed.

Solution: The Braintrust has guided Pixar through numerous storytelling challenges, ensuring that each film maintains the studio's high standards of creativity and emotional depth.

Impact: Pixar's consistent success in animation and story-telling underlines the value of building a supportive critique system. It's a model that illustrates how collaborative environments can drive collective achievement and maintain a culture of continuous improvement.

```
Pro Tip: Establish your version of a Braintrust.
Gather a circle of trusted advisors whose expertise
and honesty can help refine your vision and
strategies.
```

Exercise: Cultivating Your Supportive Environment

Mentorship Mapping:

1. List industry leaders or peers you admire and would like guidance from.
2. Craft personalized messages to request mentorship or advice.
3. Schedule regular check-ins or updates to keep mentors engaged in your progress.

Community Engagement:

1. Commit to attending or hosting regular networking events to expand your circle.
2. Participate in or create online forums related to your industry for knowledge exchange and support.

3. Initiate or join collaborative projects that align with your business goals and values.

Supportive Workspace Design:

1. Evaluate your workspace to ensure it promotes productivity and well-being.
2. Incorporate elements that inspire you, such as art, motivational quotes, or plants.
3. If possible, create spaces that encourage collaboration and casual interaction among team members or fellow entrepreneurs.

Challenge For You: Over the next three months, focus on actively building and engaging with your supportive environment. Document the impact of these efforts on your business and personal growth.

Conclusion:

The cultivation of a supportive environment is an investment that pays dividends in the form of resilience, inspiration, and growth. By intentionally building relationships with mentors, peers, and creating a nurturing physical space, you pave a path filled with valuable insights, unwavering support, and limitless possibilities. Remember, the environment you create today shapes the success you enjoy tomorrow.

11

Integrating Personal Development with Entrepreneurship

"Develop a passion for learning. If you do, you will never cease to grow."
— Anthony J. D'Angelo

A t the heart of every entrepreneurial venture lies the essence of personal development—a journey that intertwines seamlessly with the path of creating and nurturing a business. This final chapter explores the deep, interconnected relationship between an entrepreneur's personal growth and their business success. It reveals how the principles of personal development, such as self-awareness, resilience, and continuous learning, are not just complementary but integral to entrepreneurial achievement. The synergy between developing oneself and growing a business creates a dynamic cycle of improvement and innovation, where each aspect feeds into and amplifies the other.

In today's fast-paced and ever-changing business landscape, the ability to adapt, learn, and grow is more crucial than ever.

Entrepreneurs who commit to their personal development cultivate a mindset that embraces challenges as opportunities for growth, sees failure as a stepping stone to success, and values the continuous expansion of their knowledge and skills. This mindset becomes the foundation upon which they build businesses that are not only successful but also sustainable and adaptable to the demands of the modern world.

Moreover, personal development empowers entrepreneurs to lead with authenticity, empathy, and a clear vision, inspiring those around them to embark on their own journeys of growth. It fosters environments where innovation thrives, teams are motivated, and cultures of continuous improvement are nurtured. By integrating personal development strategies into their entrepreneurial endeavors, business leaders can unlock their full potential, driving their companies forward with insight, creativity, and resilience.

Opening Anecdote: Sheryl Sandberg: Growth at the Intersection of Personal and Professional

Sheryl Sandberg's journey at Facebook and her advocacy for women's leadership highlight the pivotal role personal growth plays in navigating the complexities of the business world. Through her experiences, Sandberg exemplifies how self-improvement and professional achievements can mutually enhance each other, driving impactful change and success

> ### Quick Thought:
> *The fusion of personal development with entrepreneurship catalyzes a cycle of growth, where each element*

amplifies the other.

Entrepreneurship in Action: Key Ingredients

- **Continuous Learning:** Commit to lifelong learning as a cornerstone of both personal growth and business innovation.
- **Emotional Mastery:** Cultivate emotional intelligence to navigate the highs and lows of the entrepreneurial journey with grace.
- **Purposeful Networking:** Build a network that supports and challenges you, fostering both personal and professional development.

Case Study: Brené Brown and the Power of Vulnerability in Leadership

Background: Dr. Brené Brown, a research professor and author, has significantly impacted the world with her exploration of vulnerability, courage, empathy, and leadership. Her work emphasizes the importance of personal growth in developing effective, empathetic leadership and building resilient organizations.

Approach: Through her studies, Brown discovered that vulnerability is not a weakness but a strength, especially in entrepreneurship and leadership. She advocates for leaders to embrace vulnerability to create a culture of openness, innovation, and trust. Her teachings encourage entrepreneurs to engage in deep self-reflection, understand their emotional triggers, and foster genuine connections with their teams.

Solution: By applying Brown's principles, entrepreneurs can cultivate a growth mindset that values continuous learning, authenticity, and emotional intelligence. This approach not only enhances personal development but also elevates team dynamics and organizational culture.

Impact: Entrepreneurs who embrace vulnerability and personal growth, as Brown suggests, often see a transformation in their leadership style. This shift leads to more cohesive teams, innovative problem-solving, and a supportive environment that thrives on mutual respect and understanding.

```
Pro Tip: Regularly schedule time for self-reflection
and learning. Use this time to assess your growth,
set new goals, and identify learning opportunities
that align with your entrepreneurial vision.
```

Exercise: Fusing Personal Growth with Entrepreneurial Aspirations

Growth Goal Setting:

1. Outline personal development goals that directly support your entrepreneurial vision.
2. Identify key skills that will amplify your business success and plan steps for their acquisition.
3. Recognize mindset barriers to your entrepreneurial growth and devise strategies to overcome them.

Developmental Networking:

1. Seek relationships with individuals who embody where you aspire to be in your personal and entrepreneurial journey.
2. Actively participate in or establish communities that foster mutual growth and learning.
3. Engage in mentorship, both as a mentor and a mentee, to deepen your understanding and broaden your perspective.

Integrative Practices:

1. Dedicate a portion of your day to learning, whether through reading, podcasts, or courses, focusing on topics that advance both personal and business growth.
2. Maintain a journal to track your progress, insights, and reflections on integrating personal development with entrepreneurship.
3. Incorporate wellness practices into your routine, recognizing that a healthy entrepreneur is a more effective entrepreneur.

Challenge For You: For the next six months, focus on one personal development goal each month that aligns with enhancing your entrepreneurial journey. Document the process, including challenges, successes, and insights gained, and how these contribute to your business growth.

Conclusion:

The integration of personal development with entrepreneurship is not just beneficial; it's essential for sustained success and fulfillment. By committing to a journey of continuous learning, emotional intelligence, and purposeful networking, you lay the groundwork for a thriving business and a richer, more rewarding life. Embrace this holistic approach to growth, and let it be the engine that drives you towards your dreams.

Epilogue and Action Plan

Congratulations on completing this journey of personal development and productivity for entrepreneurs! Reflecting on the journey through "Unlocking Efficiency: An Entrepreneur's Roadmap to Maximizing Productivity and Personal Growth," it becomes evident how personal development and entrepreneurship intertwine, creating a symbiotic pathway to success. This book has served as a comprehensive guide, exploring the critical aspects of personal growth, goal setting, effective time management, the cultivation of a resilient and growth-oriented mindset, and strategies for enhancing productivity—all through the lens of entrepreneurial ambition.

Key Concepts Recap:

- **Personal Development for Entrepreneurial Success:** The cornerstone of entrepreneurial success lies in continuous personal development. By embracing a growth mindset, refining leadership and communication skills, and nurturing self-awareness and emotional intelligence, you set a strong foundation for your journey.
- **Goal Setting and Management:** The art of setting and managing goals using the SMART framework underscores the importance of clarity, review, and adaptability in your entrepreneurial endeavors.

- **Time Management Techniques:** Mastering your time through prioritization, productivity tools, and techniques like the Pomodoro Technique or time blocking, empowers you to achieve more in less time.
- **Cultivating the Right Mindset:** A resilient and growth-oriented mindset is pivotal for navigating the entrepreneurial landscape, transforming challenges into opportunities for growth.
- **Stress Management and Work-Life Balance:** Essential to long-term success, managing stress and maintaining a healthy work-life balance ensure sustainability and well-being.
- **Productivity Hacks and Tools:** Leveraging the right productivity hacks and tools can significantly boost your efficiency, streamline your operations, and free up time for strategic thinking and innovation.

Your Personalized Action Plan: To integrate the insights from this book into your entrepreneurial journey, consider the following steps:

1. **Reflect on Your Growth Areas:** Identify areas for personal and professional growth. Align these with your entrepreneurial vision.
2. **Set Clear, Measurable Goals:** Develop goals that resonate with your entrepreneurial objectives. Break them into actionable milestones.
3. **Embrace Time Management:** Experiment with different time management techniques to find what best suits your style and preferences.
4. **Nurture Growth Mindset and Resilience:** Regularly

challenge yourself to step out of your comfort zone, fostering resilience and a proactive approach to learning from setbacks.

5. **Implement Stress Management Practices:** Incorporate stress-reduction strategies into your routine, prioritizing your mental and physical well-being.
6. **Leverage Productivity Enhancements:** Identify and utilize tools and hacks that streamline your workflow and enhance your productivity.
7. **Commit to Continuous Learning:** Embrace lifelong learning as a fundamental aspect of your entrepreneurial growth. Seek out new knowledge, skills, and experiences that propel you forward.

Final Reflections: "Unlocking Efficiency" was crafted to transform you into an entrepreneur capable of navigating the complexities of the business world with grace, efficiency, and innovation. The principles of personal development and productivity are not merely theoretical concepts but practical strategies for real-world application. As you move forward, remember that the journey of entrepreneurship and personal growth is continuous, filled with opportunities for learning and improvement.

The entrepreneurial landscape is ever-evolving, with new challenges and opportunities emerging at every turn. Staying adaptable, committed to growth, and proactive in your learning will be key to navigating this landscape successfully. As we close this book, let the principles of personal development, productivity, and continuous learning guide you in creating a fulfilling, successful entrepreneurial journey.

Armed with the strategies and insights from "Unlocking

Efficiency," you're now equipped to step into the world of entrepreneurship with a renewed focus on efficiency, growth, and personal development. Here's to your success, growth, and the remarkable journey that lies ahead. Let this be just the beginning of a path marked by achievement, fulfillment, and continuous evolution.

Let's embark on this transformative journey together, unlocking the full potential of your entrepreneurial spirit and scaling to new heights of success.

The Ask

Dear Entrepreneurial Trailblazer,

As we conclude our adventure through "Unlocking Efficiency: An Entrepreneur's Roadmap," I hope the journey has sparked a transformation, arming you with the insights to enhance your productivity and personal growth. This guide was designed to be your compass, navigating you towards streamlined success and operational brilliance.

If "Unlocking Efficiency" has lit your way, consider sharing your journey with a review on Amazon. Your insights illuminate the path for others, fostering a community where growth and efficiency thrive. Whether you discovered a new perspective, found clarity, or have suggestions, your input is a beacon for fellow trailblazers.

Continue your quest for excellence on my Amazon author page (https://www.amazon.com/author/patrickhperrine) where more insights await. Together, let's build a legacy of progress and collective wisdom, elevating our entrepreneurial spirits to new heights.

Thank you for your trust and fellowship on this enlightening journey.

Patrick H. Perrine

About the Author

Patrick H. Perrine is a trailblazing author, mentor, and seasoned entrepreneur with a spirit that exemplifies the essence of entrepreneurship. From his humble beginnings as a paperboy in Minnesota to his emergence as a globally recognized industry leader, his journey epitomizes resilience and determination.

Fueled by an insatiable thirst for knowledge, Patrick opted for university over his senior high school year, setting the stage for his relentless pursuit of personal growth. His tenure with UpStart, an organization championing educational opportunities for first-generation Americans, ignited his lifelong commitment to empowering others, extending beyond business and into his early philanthropic endeavors.

In his twenties, Patrick served as a Founding Board member for The Point Foundation, the largest LGBTQ scholarship foundation today. His dedication to fostering inclusivity and aiding LGBTQ students in higher education continues to positively impact hundreds of lives.

Patrick's entrepreneurial journey took flight with myPartner.com, an online dating service that addressed a critical gap in the market. Recognized as one of the "Best Matchmakers" and "Most Innovative Online Dating Sites" by the iDate Industry, the venture earned a Certificate of Recognition issued by California Legislature Assemblyman Mark Leno. This marked Patrick's first step in a journey filled with identifying unique opportunities and delivering transformative solutions across industries from skincare to dog tech.

Despite the hurdles encountered, Patrick's determination only amplified. His passion for nurturing startups led him to establish Rincon Hill Advisors. During this period, he served as a Steering Committee member for StartOut, a leading nonprofit fostering queer entrepreneurship, and consulted with Fortune 500 companies like Berkshire Hathaway and Intuit.

Adding to his achievements as an entrepreneur, Patrick became an angel investor. His foresight led him to invest in promising startups like MisterB&B, the world's largest gay hotelier, and Roadster, the leading commerce platform for car buying. His dog tech venture, too, gained recognition, leading to his selection as a NGLCC Pitch Finalist and participant in the Seamless IoT Accelerator, earning a $100,000 investment offer as a program graduate.

Most recently, Patrick served as an Entrepreneur in Residence (EiR) with 500 StartUps, an organization committed to uplifting global economies through entrepreneurship. This role solidified his dedication to guiding and uplifting aspiring entrepreneurs.

With multiple books to his credit, including recent works "Fail Fast, Recover Faster", "Ignite Your Dream", and "Fueling the Fire," Patrick continues to share his journey and insights. His writing reflects his unwavering commitment to guiding entrepreneurs through their unique journeys.

Patrick H. Perrine is more than a summary of his accomplishments. He stands as a testament to the power of determination, innovation, and a generous spirit. His contributions have been acknowledged in global press publications such as Forbes, Advocate, and Mirror, but his most profound impact lies in the lives of the entrepreneurs he's guided, inspired, and empowered. As he continues sharing his wisdom in the 10 volume series "Be A Unicorn: The New Entrepreneur's Ultimate Guide to Success," Patrick personifies the quintessential entrepreneurial journey—one of resilience, innovation, and the relentless pursuit of personal growth.

Subscribe to my newsletter:

✉ https://patrickperrine.com

Also by Patrick H. Perrine

Your next adventure in entrepreneurship awaits! Choose your guidebook on Amazon (https://www.amazon.com/author/patrickhperrine) or **www.PatrickPerrine.com**, and ignite the spark that takes your venture to new heights. The future is yours to shape!

Unicorn Rising: Ascending to the Pinnacle of Entrepreneurship and the Billionaire's Club

Fueled by entrepreneurial dreams and the allure of the Unicorn Club? Patrick H. Perrine is your guide, offering an unparalleled roadmap set to be every entrepreneur's playbook.

"Unicorn Rising" emerges as the cornerstone of the *Be A Unicorn* series, laying the groundwork that "Unlocking Efficiency" and the other nine volumes build upon.

This seminal work provides an in-depth exploration into the entrepreneurial journey, offering a comprehensive roadmap for those aiming to scale their ventures to the heights of the Unicorn Club.

Driven by the dream of entrepreneurial excellence and a place in the Unicorn Club? Patrick H. Perrine offers an unmatched guide, positioning this book as the ultimate playbook for entrepreneurs.

Within "Unicorn Rising," readers will find a guide not just to achieving lofty valuations, but to navigating the realms of innovation, transformative leadership, and enduring success It offers insights into the nuances of leadership, the forefront of emerging technologies, financial mastery, and the core of impactful entrepreneurship.

This series acknowledges the uniqueness of each entrepreneurial journey. Patrick delivers foundational wisdom alongside practical tools, emphasizing the tailored path each startup must navigate. Whether you're just beginning your entrepreneurial quest or are a seasoned professional fine-tuning your strategy, this book, and its series, light the way.

Step forward, challenge the status quo, and with "Unicorn Rising," ascend to unprecedented heights in your entrepreneurial venture.

Ignite Your Dream: The Quintessential Checklist for Aspiring Entrepreneurs
Ignite Your Dream: The Quintessential Checklist for Aspiring Entrepreneurs" by Patrick H. Perrine is an immersive guide lighting the path towards entrepreneurial success.

This power-packed handbook propels you from dreaming to achieving with a carefully curated 100-step map. Dive into real-life entrepreneur stories, extract wisdom, and utilize actionable checklists. This book transcends theoretical guidelines, providing a mentorship experience designed to turn dreams into reality.

Ready to kindle your entrepreneurial spirit? "Ignite your Dream" is your step forward towards unlocking potential and achieving success in the exciting world of entrepreneurship.

Fail Fast, Recover Faster: Bouncing Back From Entrepreneurial Failure

Embrace failure and bounce back stronger with "Fail Fast, Recover Faster: Bouncing Back From Entrepreneurial Failure". It's your guidebook through the tumultuous journey of entrepreneurship, celebrating stumbles as stepping stones towards success.

Dive into compelling tales of triumphant entrepreneurs, learn how to pivot rapidly, manage fallout, and convert setbacks into launchpads. Discover strategies for repairing financial, relationship, and reputation damage, and see your failures as badges of resilience.

This transformative book readies you to rebound from failure swiftly, turning your setbacks into your next entrepreneurial triumph. With "Fail Fast, Recover Faster", you're poised to harness your own unicorn moment and turn failure into a launching pad for success.

Fueling the Fire: Nurturing Resilience and Preventing Burnout in Entrepreneurship

In "Fueling the Fire: Nurturing Resilience and Preventing Burnout in Entrepreneurship," seasoned entrepreneur Patrick H. Perrine guides you through the entrepreneurial journey, sharing practical strategies for maintaining resilience and passion.

Drawing from 20 years of startup experience, Perrine covers everything from ideation to acquisition. Discover how to build a support system, manage your time effectively, cultivate a positive work culture, and align your work with your values.

Whether you're an experienced entrepreneur or just beginning, "Fueling the Fire" is a must-read for maintaining balance and fulfillment in the dynamic world of entrepreneurship.